OGRES

LUTHER CROSS

Cavendish Square
New York

CREATURES OF FANTASY

OGRES

BY

LUTHER CROSS

CAVENDISH SQUARE PUBLISHING · NEW YORK

Published in 2016 by Cavendish Square Publishing, LLC
243 5th Avenue, Suite 136, New York, NY 10016

First Edition

Website: cavendishsq.com

CPSIA Compliance Information: Batch #WS15CSQ

All websites were available and accurate when this book was sent to press.

Library of Congress Cataloging-in-Publication Data

Cross, Luther.
Ogres / Luther Cross.
pages cm. — (Creatures of fantasy)
Includes bibliographical references and index.
ISBN 978-1-50260-504-7 (hardcover) ISBN 978-1-50260-505-4 (ebook)
1. Ghouls and ogres—Juvenile literature. I. Title.

GR560.C76 2016
398.21—dc23

2014050255

Editorial Director: David McNamara
Editor: Kristen Susienka
Copy Editor: Rebecca Rohan
Art Director: Jeffrey Talbot
Designer: Joseph Macri
Senior Production Manager: Jennifer Ryder-Talbot
Production Editor: Renni Johnson
Photo Research: J8 Media

The photographs in this book are used by permission and through the courtesy of: Public Domain/Leutemann or Offterdinger, photo by Harke/File:Der kleine Daumling (2).jpg/Wikimedia Commons, cover; George Cruikshank/HowardTilton Memorial Library, Tulane University, 2; Crysse/Moment/ Getty Images, 6; Public Domain/Alexander Zick/File:Däumling.jpg/Wikimedia Commons, 7; AF archive/Alamy, 8; Hulton Archive/Getty Images, 11; FrankvandenBergh.iStock.com, 14; Stefan Auth/ImageBROKER/Superstock, 16; Universal Images Group/Getty Images, 19; Public Domain/Web Gallery of Art/File:Giulio Romano - Polyphemus - WGA09572.jpg /Wikimedia Commons. 21; J.R. Skelton/File:Stories of beowulf grendel.jpg/Wikimedia Commons, 23; Universal History Archive/UIG/Bridgeman Art Library, 24; Public Domain/Marina Warner/No Go The Bogeyman/File:Warner Mole Illustration.jpg/Wikimedia Commons, 28; Wolfgang Kaehler/LightRocket/Getty Images, 29; Album/Prisma/Newscom, 30; Public Domain/File:Kot w butach (Artur Oppman) page 0010a.png/Wikimedia Commons, 33; Culture Club/Getty Images, 35; Public Domain/File:D'Aulnoy.jpg/Wikimedia Commons, 38; Culture Club/Hulton Archive/Getty Images, 40; Helen Hotson/Shutterstock.com, 43; Public Domain/Walter Crane/File:Walter Crane King Arthur and the Giant Book I, Canto VIII.jpg/Wikimedia Commons, 44; Westend61/Superstock, 45; JolieBlanc/File:Mizokuchi-oni.JPG/ Wikimedia Commons, 46; Interfoto/Age Fotostock, 48; Public Domain/Walters Art Museum/File:Indian - Rama Destroys Ogress - Walters W888.jpg/ Wikimedia Commons, 49; Keystone Pictures USA/Alamy, 52; Ronald Grant Archive/Alamy, 54; AP Images, 57; RestonImages/Shutterstock.com, 59.

Printed in the United States of America

CONTENTS

INTRODUCTION

A knight faces a fearsome ogre!

Since the first humans walked Earth, myths and legends have engaged minds and inspired imaginations. Ancient civilizations used stories to explain phenomena in the world around them: the weather, tides, and natural disasters. As different cultures evolved, so too did their stories. From their traditions and observations emerged creatures with powerful abilities, mythical intrigue, and their own origins. Sometimes, different cultures encouraged various manifestations of the same creature. At other times, these creatures and cultures morphed into entirely new beings with greater powers than their predecessors.

Today, societies still celebrate the folklore of their ancestors—in films such as *The Hobbit, Maleficent,* and *X-Men*; and in stories such as *Harry Potter* and *The Lightning Thief.* Some even believe these creatures truly existed, and continue to walk the earth as living creatures. Others resign these beings to myth.

In the Creatures of Fantasy series, we celebrate captivating stories of the past from all around the world. Each book focuses on creatures both familiar and unknown: the cunning leprechaun, the valorous Pegasus, the cursed werewolf, and the covetous ogre. Their various incarnations throughout history are brought to life. All have their own

Children taunt an ogre.

origins, their own legends, and their own influences on the imagination today. Each story adds a new perspective to the human experience, and encourages people to revisit tales of the past in order to understand their presence in the modern age.

THE OGRE WAS NO COLOSSUS

"Oh my God, how ugly he was!"

GIAMBATTISTA BASILE, "THE STORY OF THE GHUL," PAGE 12

LEGENDS OF FANTASY CREATURES HAVE existed since the arrival of the first **sentient** humans. Long before words were written down, humans passed stories from generation to generation through the art of storytelling. These tales told of mythical beasts, invisible fairies, and immense giants. Among the creatures arose the ogre, a harrowing monster with staggering strength and a horrifying appearance. In recent decades, the tale of the ogre has been immortalized in popular culture, most notably through the 2001 DreamWorks film *Shrek*. One of the movie's first encounters with its **protagonist**, Shrek, goes like this:

Opposite: Shrek makes a bold attempt to scare Donkey.

"Do you know what that thing can do to you?" asks a peasant.

"He'll grind your bones for his bread," replies another.

"Yes, well, actually, that would be a giant," says the ogre, who has suddenly appeared behind them. "Now ogres, they're much worse. They'll make a suit from your freshly peeled skin. They'll shave your liver. Squeeze the jelly from your eyes. Actually, it's quite good on toast."

The peasants are frozen with fear. They have never actually seen an ogre.

In the opening scene, a mob of peasants scoured the forest looking for anything that matched the description of a "fairy-tale creature." The local government had recently declared such creatures illegal and offered a reward for their capture. Shrek, being an ogre, fit the description and could have been an impressive bounty. However, the peasants quickly realized they had crossed the wrong fairy-tale creature. The story continues, sending Shrek on an epic adventure to save his swamp and homeland. The film makes many references to ogre literature and other fairy-tale creatures, and as the movie progresses, film-watchers piece together fragments of ogre lore, better understanding what an ogre is, and isn't.

Defining the Ogre

The opening scene of *Shrek* outlines one of the common confusions of fairy-tale lore: What are ogres? Are they not giants? Ellen Phillips made this distinction in her book, *The Enchanted World: Giants and Ogres,* in a passage about a nameless tale of a miller and an ogre: "The giant was no colossus. He was only a few feet taller than a man, but he was immensely strong in the manner of all those with giants'

Polyphemus the Cyclops (played by Reid Asato) in *The Odyssey* TV miniseries

blood. Under a matted thatch of hair, his face was wart-covered and twisted. The miller, repulsed by this and all too aware of the power in his heavy muscles, gave him the contemptuous name of Ogre." Such a definition is synonymous with the average person's understanding of an ogre, but this is only the first "layer of the onion," as Shrek would say, that needs to be peeled away to fully understand what it means to be an ogre.

From *Encyclopedia Britannica*'s entry on ogres: "[One] who devours humans is a form of ogre. The idea of the ogre can also be seen, more broadly, in a metaphoric sense in literature ... [such] as ... a political tyrant or dictator who controls and exploits others and in a sense swallows them up."

Thus, the ogre has found itself in a complex place in fairy-tale history. As will be explored in further chapters, an ogre can be a Shrek, a squat green monster. It can be a giant, insofar as it can be larger than the average human, though it is rarely as big as the Cyclops in Homer's *Odyssey*. It can also be a demon whose form has been derived from some heinous fate, usually as punishment for a grave deed or indulgence. Marina Warner, in her book *No Go the Bogeyman: Scaring, Lulling, and Making Mock*, describes one definition of ogre:

> Fully invested with classical and Christian anthropophagic and hellish traits, the ogres of fairy tales ... become roundly comic, and their downfall is contemplated with ebullient optimism. Whatever their might and their magic, they meet their match in the stories' hero (sometimes heroine) and fail to assuage their ravenous hunger. There is a humour and gratification ... in imagining ogres, in contemplating the

outrageous scope of their desires, as well as watching the spectacle of their ultimate defeat.

She goes on to claim that, "the bestial, the lowly, the disfigured are redeemed when the heroine—or hero—arrives at a fresh understanding of an ogre's true nature." Here, Warner is writing about ogres as they appear in the works of Italian writer Giambattista Basile, whose work will be discussed at greater length in a coming chapter. However, what Warner writes is only the tip of the iceberg. When examining the ogre as it appears in folklore around the world, one will find many meanings, characteristics, and metaphors. This book will discuss some of the most explored ogre legends, and examine how many portrayals only give the reader a fraction of what this creature was believed to be.

From these examinations, one may come to find that ogres are not all of what they might seem or have been portrayed as. As happens with most fairy tales, throughout the ages, the ogre's shape, characteristics, and interactions with others has evolved. Modern culture portrays ogres in quite a different way than in times past. The ogre, like so many other creatures, has become something reinvented. Its modern portrayal is a mixture of past traits and new.

Before examining modern-day representations of ogres, however, one must first come to understand earlier representations of the creature, how it existed in literature, and what it symbolized for earlier cultures.

Storytellers in sub-Saharan Africa often told their stories to family members inside their homes.

Will the Real Ogre Please Stand Up?

In Kenya, there is the legend of "Kiondondoe and the Ogre." Kiondondoe was a very gullible little girl. If her grandmother said, "Do not give food to strangers," she would surely do it, at her own expense, and starve all day. If her grandmother said, "Don't open the door for anyone," she would.

One day, her grandmother left her alone in the house. An ogre came to the door and knocked. The door was locked, but Kiondondoe let him in. No sooner had she opened the door than the ogre snatched her up and put her in his bag. The ogre used the girl to beg for food from other homes. One day they came upon a woman who pulled a switcheroo on the ogre:

So he told the woman to keep his bag for him while he visited the bush for a little while. When the ogre had gone to the bush, the woman took Kiondondoe out of the bag quickly and hid her. She then put a stone in that bag. When the ogre came back and she gave him his bag, he asked, "How come it has become so heavy?" The woman told the ogre, "Ah! You ogre! Don't you know that when a load is put down it always becomes heavier?" The ogre took his bag, saying, "Oh! Yes! When a load is put down it becomes heavier. That is good because today is when this meat of mine will be eaten."

When the ogre returned to his tribe, he boasted that tonight they would eat Kiondondoe, who had been properly fattened up. He had them gather firewood and build a fire. However, when the other ogres went to fetch Kiondondoe, they found only the stone. Furious, they grabbed the first ogre and threw him into the fire, having decided to feast on him instead.

2

AN OGREVIEW

"The monster of evil fiercely did harass,
The ill-planning death-shade, both elder and younger,
Trapping and tricking them. He trod every night then
The mist-covered moor-fens; men do not know where
Witches and wizards wander and ramble."

Beowulf, trans. Lesslie Hall

THROUGHOUT HISTORY, MANY CULTURES have classified ogres, first and foremost, as monsters. They are known for their ferocious looks and demeanors, and their hunger for human flesh. Moreover, their appearance in literature since early times has secured the creature as one of folklore and fantasy. The ogre is a creature with many attributes and its own personality, separate from other monsters in its genre. Often confused with similar enormous beings, such as Titans, giants, and trolls, ogres are, in fact, a unique species, different from their contemporaries. Many cultures have given traits to the ogre that still exist in modern-day representations. However, the earliest occurrences of ogre lore were recorded as far back as the 1600s,

Opposite: The Mouth of Orcus, carved in stone in the Gardens of Bomarzo, Italy

and the first writers of these creatures were the instigators of what would become legend.

Ogre's Origins

The origins of the ogre date back to seventeenth-century France, when moral fairy tales were being written. The earliest recorded use of the word in English was in 1713 and is considered to be derived from the Latin word *Orcus*, who was the Roman god of the underworld. Orcus's own origins are a bit conflated, but he was often presented in art and literature as a giant, hairy beast.

Little distinction has been made throughout history between ogres and giants. This was in part because of the incorrect assumption in early times that Orcus was synonymous with the Cyclops, a one-eyed monster, who is often presented as a giant himself. However, ogres have one distinguishing characteristic that sets them apart from their gigantic brethren: a taste for the flesh and blood of infants and children.

Two of the earliest accounts of ogres come from French author Charles Perrault (1628–1703). Perrault was a pioneer of a new tradition of the time: the fairy tale. These morals, meant for children but enjoyed by adults in bourgeois Parisian circles of the time, came to be known as "fairy tales" with the publication of Madame d'Aulnoy's *Les Contes des Fées* (*The Fairy Tales*) in 1697. That same year, Perrault published his own book, *Histoires ou contes du temps passé, avec des moralitès: contes de ma mère l'Oye*, or *Histories or Tales of Long Ago with Morals: Tales of Mother Goose*. It contained eight of what are now considered classic examples of the fairy tale, two of which featured an ogre as the main **antagonist**: "Puss-in-Boots" and "Hop o' My Thumb."

While Perrault may be responsible for bringing the ogre into the consciousness of modern readers, there are certainly examples of ogre-like creatures that predate him. In fact, there is a direct lineage between "Puss-in-Boots" and "The Tales of the Ogre" written by Italian author Giambattista Basile in the mid-seventeenth century. His book, *Lo cunto de li cunti overo lo trattenemiento de peccerille*, or *The Tale of Tales*, or *Entertainment for Little Ones*, was the first collection of Italian fairy tales on record. His collection is more commonly known by the title *Il Pentamerone*. The first edition was published posthumously in two volumes by his sister, Adriana Basile, under the pseudonym Gian Alesio Abbatutis in 1634 and 1636.

Giambattista Basile, the godfather of both the modern fairy tale and the ogre

The impact of *Il Pentamerone* was overshadowed by contemporaries such as Perrault because it was written in Neapolitan, a dialect of Italian native to Basile that was considered difficult to translate at the time. Further complicating matters was the nature of the prose itself: it was densely worded and heavily metaphorical. Basile's love of baroque stylings may have cost him his place as creator of the modern ogre myth.

The Importance of Giants

Ancient stories often confused ogres with giants. This is because giants themselves are almost "proto-ogres." Their lineage is much older, spanning far into prehistory. In a sense, they laid the groundwork for the ogre. They too were hideous, large, and man-eating. Over time, stories of the giant portrayed them as smaller and smaller creatures. As the giant "shrank" in size to become the modern ogre, so did his

Il Pentamerone's "Tales of the Ogre"

Giambattista Basile's *Il Pentamerone* was not immediately translated into any other language. It was by no means inaccessible, but did remain obscure for centuries. While the Brothers Grimm, famous for their chronicles of fairy tales from around the world, praised it as an inspiration for their works, it was not translated into English until the nineteenth century. One of these translations was by Sir Richard Francis Burton and published by Henry & Co., London, in 1893. This edition maintained the two-volume arrangement of Adriana Basile's initial Italian publication. However, one distinct difference was the use of the word "ghul" (an archaic form of *ghoul*) in place of "ogre" in the collection's opening tale: "Il cunto dell'uerco," or "The Tale of the Ogre." The modern Italian word for ogre is *orco*, an obvious descendant of the Latin *Orcus*. However, the Neopolitan word *uerco* is more complex, used to describe any creature that was large, hairy, manlike, and evil. The word almost foreshadows the different incarnations of ogres and ogresses found in folklore across the globe.

Basile's ogre is a wealthy creature who was described as such: "His head was larger than an Indian vegetable-marrow, his forehead full of bumps, his eyebrows united, his eyes crooked, his nose flat, with nostrils like a forge, his mouth open like an oven, from which protruded two tusks like unto a boar's; a hairy breast had he, and arms like reels; and bandy-legged was he, and flat-footed like a goose; briefly he was an hideous monster, frightful to behold." This was more description than other authors had given to ogres, and was very different from how an ogre might be described in other European countries. This description surely set the stage for a creature that is not quite giant, not quite man, but certainly a beast.

prey. Giants tend to feast on adults. Ogres tend to feast on children.

A very early example of the man-eating giant is the Cyclops in Homer's *Odyssey*. In book nine of the Greek epic, Odysseus, the protagonist, came upon the island of the Cyclopes, which is thought to be Sicily. While exploring, he and his men came upon a cave that was full of provisions. What they did not realize was that this cave was home to one of the island's famed Cyclopes, Polyphemus. A sheep farmer by trade, Polyphemus was very nasty in temperament and so angered by his intruders that he trapped them all inside the cave and proceeded to eat them in pairs.

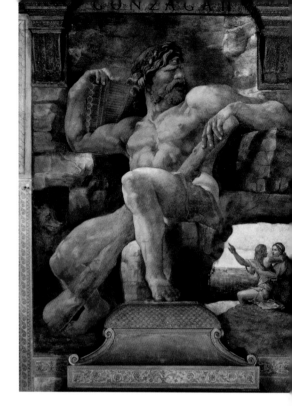

Polyphemus as depicted by Giulio Romano

Odysseus came up with a plan to subdue their captor. He carried with him a potent red wine given to him as a gift, or ***xenia***, by Maron, a "priest of Apollo, guardian god of Ismarus." The concept of xenia is a recurring theme in the Odyssey and plays an important role in Odysseus conquering Polyphemus. Odysseus narrates:

> I went up to him, holding an ivy-wood bowl full of dark wine, and said: "Here, Cyclops, have some wine to follow your meal of human flesh, so you can taste the sort of drink we carried in our ship. I was bringing the drink to you as a gift, hoping you might pity me and help me on my homeward path: but your savagery is past bearing. Cruel man, why would anyone on earth ever visit you again, when you behave so badly?"

At this, [Polyphemus] took the cup and drained it, and found the sweet drink so delightful he asked for another draught: "Give me more, freely, then quickly tell me your name so I may give you a guest gift, one that will please you. Among us Cyclopes the fertile earth produces rich grape clusters, and Zeus' rain swells them: but this is a taste from a stream of ambrosia and nectar."

Odysseus replied that his name was "Nobody." As soon as Polyphemus passed out from drinking the wine, Odysseus took a wooden spear and punctured his captor's eye, blinding him. When the giant called out for help, he yelled, "Nobody, my friends, is trying to kill me by violence or treachery." The friends who heard him replied, "If you are alone, and nobody does you violence, it's an inescapable sickness that comes from Zeus: pray to the Lord Poseidon, our father." Polyphemus did not get the help he needed and Odysseus and his crew escaped.

What makes Polyphemus notable in the lineage of the ogre is that he was not only deformed and man-eating, but covetous as well. Moreover, while he may not have had more than other Cyclopes of the land, Polyphemus had what Odysseus and his mates were looking for: food and shelter. Ogres, too, are often seen as those who have. The humans who encounter them are those who have not.

A Missing Link?

While defining the exact evolution of the ogre throughout early history may be difficult, there is one creature that could be considered an important missing link: Grendel, a villain in the Anglo-Saxon epic *Beowulf*. The poem, whose author and original

title are unknown, was discovered in modern times in a collection of ancient manuscripts composed around the eighth century CE. The story tells of Beowulf, the hero, who finds himself pitted against Grendel, a monster, at the behest of Hrothgar, a Danish king. Grendel has been terrorizing Hrothgar and his kingdom for some time.

Evidence that Grendel could be a relative of the ogre is seen in several character descriptions. First, he is a monster with a hideous appearance. Next, he does eat people, attacking soldiers in the night. While pure ogres usually eat children, in some literary tales, ogres have eaten adults. Finally, Grendel's place in society, as a monster alienated from civilization, likewise seems a trait of ogres.

The fearsome Grendel on the hunt

Some scholars also see Grendel in a metaphorical sense. According to *Encyclopedia Britannica*, "Many … have seen Grendel as the embodiment of the physical and moral evil of heathenism. Beowulf's struggles to overcome the monster are thought to symbolize Anglo-Saxon England's emerging Christianity."

The first ogres may not have physically appeared until the 1600s; however, their ancestors lived rich lives in the history of literature, and gave rise to the creatures we know today. As ogre legends took hold in societies, there were certain stories that captivated audiences and truly defined ogres for the world.

THE OGRE THAT CONSUMES US

"At last there came to this trial an ogre who was the most ugly being in the world, the very sight of whom would make the boldest man tremble and quake with fear."

GIAMBATTISTA BASILE, "THE FLEA"

WHEN YOU THINK OF AN OGRE, WHAT comes to mind? A ferocious man-eater? A monster with a keen sense of smell? Perhaps the words "fee fie foe fum," the classic phrase from the English fairy tale "Jack and the Beanstalk." If you thought of any of these, you're thinking of ogres. Surprised by the last part? Many people usually think these words were spoken by a giant, but early written versions of the story were known to depict the monster as an ogre.

The ogre's form has taken on many different transformations throughout its existence in folklore. Unlike a vampire, which can change its shape at will, and unlike a werewolf, whose shape changes against its will, the ogre is permanently deformed. Whether as

Opposite: An Irish political cartoon featuring a politician as a man-eating ogre.

tall as a tree or as squat as a grandmother, the ogre's ugliness or deformity remains constant. It does not exhibit powers like other monsters or gods. Rather, its powers come from forces outside its control. The form of the ogre is usually the result of its own experiences in the world.

CREATURE OF GREED

At the core of the ogre's dilemma is consumption. Across the world, folklore and fairy tales containing ogres show the creature as a hoarder of wealth, or a greedy humanoid whose disfigurement is the result of an obsession with either an individual or object. Basile's "The Flea" from *Il Pentamerone* tells the story of a king who raises a flea to be as large, or larger, than a sheep. He then slaughters the flea, presents its skin to the public, and decrees that if anyone should guess the origin of the skin, they can have his daughter's hand in marriage. Of course, the only one who gets it right is the town's wealthy and hideous ogre. Honoring his word, the king allows his daughter, Porziella, to be taken away. The pair sets off to the ogre's lair:

> Poor Porziella, seeing herself thus caught in the net, with the face of a person condemned to death, with the heart of one whose head is lying between the ax and the block, took the hand of the ogre, who dragged her off without any attendants to the wood where the trees made a palace for the meadow to prevent its being discovered by the sun, and the brooks murmured, having knocked against the stones in the dark, while the wild beasts wandered where they liked without paying toll, and went safely through the thicket whither no man ever came unless he had lost his way. Upon

this spot, which was as black as an unswept chimney, stood the ogre's house ornamented all round with the bones of the men whom he had devoured. Think but for a moment of the horror of it to the poor girl.

But this was nothing at all in comparison with what was to come.

Before dinner she had peas and after dinner parched beans. Then the ogre went out to hunt and returned home laden with the quarters of the men whom he had killed, saying, "Now, wife, you cannot complain that I don't take good care of you; here is a fine store of eatables, take and make merry and love me well, for the sky will fall before I will let you want for food."

The ogre in this tale is hardly different from his peers. He consumes humans obsessively, and even decorates his house with their leftovers like trophies.

However, ogres are very specific in their diet. They eat only men, male children, and babies of both genders. Adult women usually come out unscathed, as they are seen as prizes, not dinner. An ogre, if unmarried, desires the beauty of a fair princess.

In "The Flea," an old woman takes pity on the princess and sends her eight sons to rescue her. The brothers have special powers that can be used against her oppressor. The sons use their powers but not without challenge from the ogre:

As Ceccone [a son] was speaking the ogre came, planted his ladder and began to climb up; but Ceccone, taking aim at

him, shot out one of his eyes and laid him at full length on the ground, like a pear dropped from a tree. Then he went out of the tower and cut off the ogre's head with a big knife he carried about with him, just as if it had been new-made cheese.

The sons return the princess to her father and are rewarded well for their service. However, the princess is married off to a suitable prince—who happens to be not one of the eight sons who had just risked his life to save her.

Examining Ogres

Looking again at Marina Warner's analysis of what an ogre "means" in *No Go the Bogeyman*, she has this to say: "death—extreme death in another's jaws—is the most obvious meaning that the ogre conveys. But the precise nature and status of that material or spiritual death changes … fairy-tale cannibals refract different motives in [a] story [depending on] when it is told and [where] it is received." Warner is reminding the reader how diverse the ogre can be and how its diversity is relevant to our unique experience and understanding of the myth. As mentioned before, the breadth and depth of ogre legendry are vast, but the shoes he fills are always quite specific.

Often in literature, however, there is one particular myth to which all other myths refer. Ogre lore differs from region to region and from era to era, yet some myths are so recognizable that they have become part of the folklore canon. Understanding these myths is also important to understanding modern-day depictions of the ogre, which is where we begin the next chapter.

Cleverness Kills the Ogre

Different parts of the world have different takes on the ogre legend. In Africa, the Sukuma people of modern-day Tanzania tell the tale of "The Clever Young Man and the Monster." In this story, an ogre named Shing'weng'we swallowed up all the people and animals of the world except for one pregnant woman. She gave birth to a son named Masala Kulangwa, which translates as "the smart or clever person who understands quickly." As he grew up, he remained determined to someday capture Shing'weng'we and kill him. He first killed a grasshopper and brought it to his mother. She informed him that, alas, no, this was not the ogre, but at least they had something to eat. Sometime later, he killed a bird, and his mother again had to tell him it was not the ogre, but at least they had something to eat. The same happened again with an antelope and gazelle. Then one day the boy found the ogre.

Some African storytellers use musical instruments like these to help tell their tales.

Being the clever young man that his name implied, he overtook the ogre and cut open his stomach. Out came the boy's father and the rest of the world's population (both human and animal). In doing so, the boy accidentally injured an old lady who, subsequently, tried to curse him, but he had the right medicine to treat her. Thusly, everyone declared that he be king. His mother got to be the queen mother. The appetite of the ogre and the sheer capacity of his stomach (not to mention his ability to keep people and animals alive) attest to the many powers an ogre can possess.

THE OGRE THAT WORKS AGAINST US

"His wife said,
'It must be the calf I have just prepared for
cooking that you smell.'
'I smell fresh flesh, I tell you,'
said the ogre, looking at his wife suspiciously."

CHARLES PERRAULT, "HOP O' MY THUMB"

I N OGRE LORE THERE ARE TWO TALES THAT introduce different concepts of ogres into fairytale literature. The first is "Puss-In-Boots"; the second is "Hop o' My Thumb." Both stories were written by Charles Perrault, a chronicler of some of the first fairy tales. From these tales others have sprung, and the ogre has morphed into the form it is known by today.

PUSS-IN-BOOTS

"Puss-in-Boots" by Charles Perrault is the tale of a nameless cat willed to the son of a farmer upon his death. Unhappy with his inheritance, the son complained loudly about his discontent. Eventually, the cat decided to chime in. He informed his master

Opposite: Puss-In-Boots calls to the King to "save" his master.

that all he needed was a satchel and a cat-sized pair of boots. If the master provided these, all his problems would be solved. The farmer's son felt he had nothing to lose and agreed.

The cat went about in his new boots and caught rabbits and partridges in his satchel. He delivered them to the King, telling him they were gifts from a mysterious Marquis de Carabas. This went on for months, and the King was always pleased with the food the cat gave him. The cat devised a plan to have the King finally meet the Marquis. One day, the cat had his owner go for a bath in a river near a bridge. He knew the King's procession would cross the bridge that day, and he would be ready when they did. The cat, on the lookout, said his owner should pretend to drown on his command.

As the King's carriage crossed the bridge, he saw the cat's owner drowning and had his driver stop. He commanded his guards to save the man. Once his owner was safely ashore, the cat lied to the King and said that his master, the Marquis de Carabas, had had his clothes stolen. The King recognized the cat and was grateful for the gifts, and so commanded that his guards clothe the man in his best available garments. Once dressed, the Marquis was introduced to the King's daughter, who was considered to be the fairest lady of the land.

The King requested the Marquis ride with them to a nearby castle. The cat, moving swiftly, went on ahead and commanded the peasants he met to answer that their land was owned by the Marquis if asked. He then went to the castle of the true owner of the land, a nameless ogre, and requested to see him. The cat had heard the ogre could turn into any creature he imagined. Once granted an audience with him, the cat challenged the ogre to prove

The King heeds
Puss-In-Boots's call.

he could change his form at will. Accepting the challenge, the ogre
turned into a lion and frightened the cat so much that he retreated
to the rafters. The cat then dared the ogre to prove his abilities
further by changing into a much smaller creature, such as a mouse.
The ogre obliged, and the cat swiftly pounced and gobbled him up.
Soon the King's procession reached the castle. They were greeted
by the cat, who welcomed his master home.

A Difference of Ogres

In "Puss-in-Boots," the ogre was not the eater but the eaten. This differs from other ogre stories, which usually feature children or other humans as victims and ogres as villains. In this story, the cat is in fact the monster. He uses his cunning to trick his master, the King, and the ogre into doing his bidding. However, this theme was not something common to Perrault's ogres. Perrault's other ogre fairy tale, "Hop o' My Thumb," shows a very different ogre. It is perhaps in this tale that the motif of ogres-as-child-eaters first emerged.

Hop o' My Thumb

In the tale of "Hop o' My Thumb," there lived a woodcutter, his wife, and their seven sons in a remote forest. One of the sons was particularly small and quiet. His name was Hop o' My Thumb, which in those days described a person with his characteristics. The mother and father were no longer able to afford to feed their children and bickered over what to do. The father decided that the only answer was to leave his children behind in the woods to be eaten by wolves. The mother vehemently opposed this idea but was unable to change his mind. Little did they know, Hop had been listening.

The woodcutter led his children into the forest, but Hop was prepared. He laid a trail of tiny white stones behind them. When their father suddenly disappeared, Hop was the only one not in tears. He told his brothers to follow him home. When they returned, they overheard their parents arguing inside. It turns out that a local squire had given them ten **sovereigns** [gold coins] that afternoon, enough to feed the entire family for months. The mother exclaimed, "Where are my poor children now?" At that moment, Hop revealed that they had come home.

Hop removes the ogre's magical boot that gives him great speed.

Months passed and the family went about their lives happily, but as soon as their wealth was gone, the woodcutter and his wife conspired again to abandon their children. The woodcutter once again led his children to the same spot in the forest and, once again, Hop was ready. His parents had foreseen their smallest son's preparedness and double-locked the door to their home, prohibiting him from leaving to gather pebbles. Not so easily dissuaded, he kept a piece of daily bread in his pocket and laid crumbs upon the trail. When their father disappeared, the sons knew what to do, but they soon found Hop's efforts thwarted. Birds had come along and eaten all the crumbs.

As nighttime approached, it became clear they were lost. However, Hop was determined to lead his brothers home. He soon spotted a light in the distance. The light was coming from a house, but not theirs. Eager to get out of the rain, they knocked on the door and a woman answered. She sympathized with their plight but informed them that her husband was a child-eating ogre. Hop declared that, in spite of this, he and his brothers would be better off there than outside in the cold rain where the wolves lurked.

The ogre's wife hoped she could hide the children from her husband, but allowed them to warm themselves by the fire while he was out. As they did this, he returned home unexpectedly. Furious that the wife would try to hide children from him, he declared they would be killed immediately, but his wife convinced him that the supper she had prepared would be enough and that he should wait till morning. Reluctantly, he agreed.

The ogre's wife put Hop and his brothers to bed in the same room where their seven daughters slept. Worried the ogre would

36

get hungry for them in the middle of the night, Hop decided to switch his and his brother's hats with the gold crowns worn by the ogre's daughters. Sure enough, the ogre came into the room and slaughtered his daughters, mistaking them for the boys. After the ogre had returned to bed, Hop and his brothers escaped.

In the wee hours of the morn, the ogre and his wife realized what had happened. The ogre chased after Hop and his brothers but eventually grew tired. While the ogre rested, Hop stole his magical boots. In them, he ran swiftly back to the ogre's house and tricked his wife into giving him money to save the ogre from bandits. He then fled back to his home where he gave the good fortune to his parents, and they lived happily—and well fed—ever after.

TALES OF TWO OGRES

In the tales, both ogres were wealthy but in the end had their wealth stolen from them by the protagonist. Perrault and other contemporaries who wrote fairy tales lived very differently than their characters; however, regardless of their backgrounds, it seems the "Robin Hood"–like nature of these stories is what has allowed them to endure the centuries.

MARIE CATHERINE LE JUMEL
DE BERNEVILLE.
Comtesse d'Aulnoi.
Morte au Mois de Janvier 1705.

The Countess d'Aulnoy also told fairy tales featuring ogres.

D'Aulnoy's Fairy Tales

Perrault was not the only person to write about ogres. The first tale in *The Fairy Tale*, a collection by Madame d'Aulnoy, a contemporary of Perrault, is "The Orange Tree and the Bee." This story features a family of ogres as antagonists, and bears many similarities to "Hop o' My Thumb." It tells of an infant princess lost at sea who washes ashore on an island inhabited by ogricons, "a people that preyed upon mankind, and caught them by snares and stratagems … [and ate] them with a dog-like appetite, having mouths from one ear to the other." The island was ruled by an ogre and an ogress. The ogress hid the princess from her husband, who surely would have eaten the infant, and raised her in secret until she was old enough to be revealed.

One day, a young prince washed ashore after his ship was wrecked at sea. He was saved by the princess but eventually shown to the ogre and ogress. The princess was destined to marry their son and was now safe from the ogre's hunger. However, the same could not be said for the newly found prince. He was made to sleep in a room with other ogricons, who all wore gold crowns to bed, and the princess was sure that the ogre would eat him in the night. However, she had a plan, and tricked the ogre twice into eating his own ogricons, saving the prince. The two ran.

The ogre put on a pair of magical boots to pursue them. The princess, however, had a powerful wand that she used to turn the prince and herself into various creatures, confusing the ogre. Eventually she turned them into an orange tree and a bee, respectively.

It is unclear whether Perrault's story or d'Aulnoy's tale came first, and it would be unfair to accuse one of copying the other. However, these stories originated in the salons of Paris where authors and other socialites would meet and share stories, so it is possible they influenced each other. One possible reason why d'Aulnoy's tales were overlooked by audiences during her time was that they were written in a conversational manner and aimed at adults, not children. Perrault's stories, on the other hand, were the exact opposite and proved popular outside the salons, surviving to this day.

THE OGRE THAT WALKS AMONG US

"And Og, king of Bashan, and his whole army marched out to meet them in battle at Edrei. The Lord said to Moses, 'Do not be afraid of him, for I have handed him over to you.'"

21 NUMBERS 33-34

CONSIDERING HOW PROMINENT THE OGRE is in fairy-tale folklore, one might ask: Did such a creature ever really exist? How could it not considering the effect it has had on writers and storytellers throughout history? While the ogre today is no more realistic than a cat that wears boots, one might find the earthly origins of this creature surprising.

A BIBLICAL PRESENCE

One of the most famous religious works in the world, the Bible, tells the story of Moses, who led the Jewish people out of Egypt and founded the land of Israel. He was also given the Ten Commandments on Mount Sinai. Moses is a figure considered

Opposite: Moses may have been one of prehistory's few real-life ogre killers.

both mythological and historical and, as such, would be one of a few historical figures to have possibly come into contact with an ogre. The first five books of the Old Testament, known as the Pentateuch to Christians and the Torah to Jews, tell Moses's story. In the third chapter of the Book of Deuteronomy, Moses describes the battle he led against Og, a giant king of the Amorite city of Basan (located in modern day Syria):

> And the Lord said to me: Fear him not: because he is delivered into thy hand, with all his people and his land: and thou shalt do to him as thou hast done to Sehon king of the Amorrhites, that dwelt in Hesebon. / So the Lord our God delivered into our hands, Og … and all his people: and we utterly destroyed them, / Wasting all his cities at one time, there was not a town that escaped us: sixty cities, all the country of Argob the kingdom of Og in Basan. / All the cities were fenced with very high walls, and with gates and bars, besides innumerable towns that had no walls. / And we utterly destroyed them, as we had done to Sehon the king of Hesebon, destroying every city, men and women and children: / But the cattle and the spoils of the cities we took for our prey.

Og is later described in the Book of Amos. Moses again says, "I destroyed the Amorite [Og] before them, though he was tall as the cedars and strong as the oaks. I destroyed his fruit above and his roots below" (Amos 2:9). Accounts vary as to the size and grotesqueness of Og, but the similarity between "Og" and "ogre" cannot be ignored. The Bible claims that Moses led two million people out of Egypt, but historians argue that it could have been

St. Michael's Mount in Cornwall, England

several hundred thousand. Regardless, if this is so, couldn't Moses have fought a king not as tall as cedars but more the size of an ogre?

KING ARTHUR AND THE OGRES

In medieval times there was King Arthur. Like Moses, the historical accuracy of his life is debated, but there may also be some truth to his existence. If so, King Arthur may have had an encounter with an ogre.

Near Cornwall, England, there is a tidal island called St. Michael's Mount. In the Cornish language, it is called *Karrek Loos yn Koos*, which means the "grey rock in a wood." The island is small and the mount rises sharply upward. There is an ominous-looking castle perched at its peak. The castle is prominent in many legends, one of which involves King Arthur and a giant. In Chapter 6 of *The Legends of King Arthur and his Knights* by Sir James Knowles, Arthur was tasked with his mission to go to the castle and save his cousin's wife from a giant. There he would be rewarded with gold and other treasures.

And so Arthur gathered his knights and headed to the giant's lair. No sooner had they landed than they encountered the giant

King Arthur slays the giant of St. Michael's Mount.

who "sat at supper, gnawing on a limb of a man, and baking his huge frame by the fire, while three damsels turned three spits whereon were spitted, like larks, twelve young children lately born." Enraged by what he saw, Arthur engaged the giant in combat. The giant, Arthur realized, was strong, but no match for his sword, which knocked the giant down:

The giant, howling in great anguish, threw away his club of iron, and caught the king in both his arms and strove to crush his ribs together. But King Arthur struggled and writhed, and twisted him about, so that the giant could not hold him tightly; and as they fiercely wrestled, they both fell, and rolling over one another, tumbled—wrestling, and struggling, and fighting frantically—from rock to rock, till they came to the sea.

And as they tore and strove and tumbled, the king ever and anon smote at the giant with his dagger, till his arms stiffened in death around King Arthur's body, and groaning horribly, he died.

Once freed, Arthur commanded that the giant's head be severed and hung on the castle gates for all to see.

King Arthur is known as "the greatest of all giant slayers," but was it possible that the real Arthur fought a real giant—or perhaps an ogre? The truth may never fully be known.

The Ogre of Kindlifresserbrunnen Fountain

The Kindlifresserbrunnen statue is a work of art that predates Perrault's fairy tales of ogres. Created in 1546, this statue, which sits atop a fountain, is one of Bern, Switzerland's oldest pieces of art. It means "child eater," and for good reason: the creature is devouring a child, with others at its side, ready to suffer the same fate. The reason for the statue's existence is unknown and has sparked many theories; however, from its grotesque nature and its feast of babies, it is clear this creature is an ogre. It is not tall, as some ogres have been depicted, but very short, shorter than a human. Some people think the statue depicts the Greek Titan Kronos, who ate his children to keep any of them from taking over. Others have different ideas as to what the statue illustrates. Nevertheless, the existence of this

art piece testifies that ogres were in a part of folklore for much longer than perhaps originally considered.

THE OGRE WITHIN US

"O ogre's daughter, you whom the ogre is raising, fattening,
then in the end will devour!"

"The Ostrich and the Sultan's Son", trans. Hasan M. El-Shamy

DESPITE THEIR PROMINENCE IN EUROPE, ogre legends exist across the globe. Each culture gives a different view to the ogre, offering varying perspectives and characteristics that make the creature unique.

Onibaba of Japan

Japanese folklore is rife with **yōkai**, or "strange apparitions." One particular form of these is an **oni**, a word that could be loosely translated as "ogre" but is equally used to describe all kinds of heinous demons. One prominent oni tale is the story "**Onibaba.**"

"Onibaba" tells the tale of a quiet child born to a wealthy family in Kyoto. At five years old the girl was unable or unwilling

Opposite: This public building in Hoki, Japan, is decorated with an oni statue.

Onibaba after severing the head of an infant, but what she really wants is the poor child's liver.

to speak, despite her pleasant disposition. Her parents were devastated until, one day, her mother came upon a fortune-teller. The fortune-teller said that if they fed their daughter the fresh liver of an unborn child, she would be cured. Agreeing that this was the only option, the parents tasked their daughter's nanny with retrieving the suitable organ. Before embarking on her mission, the nanny gave her own daughter a special amulet to protect her while she was away. What became an arduous and fruitless journey took the nanny to the rural moors outside the town Adachi, called *Adachi-ga-hara* in Japanese (in present day Nihonmatsu in Fukushima Prefecture), to a cave where she decided to rest and wait for a suitable traveler to pass. Years went by to no avail, until one day a young pregnant woman walked by. The nanny wasted no time. Only after she had killed the woman and the child did she notice what the woman was wearing: the very same amulet she had given her daughter. Grieved beyond sanity, the nanny went mad and retreated into the cave where she became the oni yōkai Onibaba and feasted on the flesh of any traveler who passed by her cave.

Other tales speak of Onibaba as the "demon-hag of Adachi-ga-hara" but do not necessarily recount the specific events of this tale. Some versions claim she was ultimately killed by an arrow in a Buddhist **exorcism** ritual. It is also believed that Onibaba herself was a real creature, and she has been immortalized by a museum at Kanzeji Temple where visitors can view artifacts from her life, pray to her victims, and walk along the pond where she is said to have cleaned up after her killings.

The Ghulah of Arabia

Sir Richard Francis Burton was well known for many things, among them translating foreign language works into English. He spent much time in the Orient, having fought for England in the Crimean War and traveling to Mecca in disguise. He was one of the first people, along with John Payne, to translate *The Book of the Thousand Nights and a Night* (1885), more commonly known as *The Arabian Nights*. One tale is entitled "The Prince and the Ogress."

Other cultures, such as India, also tell stories of heroes killing ogresses.

A young prince, upon being separated from his *wazir*, or chaperone, came upon a princess. She claimed to have been separated from her traveling party as well, having fallen asleep on horseback and then fallen off. The smitten prince offered to give her a ride. They came upon an old ruin where the princess thought it would be appropriate to relieve herself. The prince granted her this pit stop and then waited, waited, and waited for her to be done. Finally, he went into the ruins to see what the holdup was. He came to find that the princess was not really a princess, but a **Ghulah**, a wicked ogress, and she was informing her ogre brood of her scheme: "'O my children, this day I bring you a fine fat youth for dinner,' whereto they answered, 'Bring him quick to us, O our mother, that we may browse upon him our bellies full.'" The Ghulah then saw the prince and threatened to cause him great harm if he didn't pay her what his life was worth. He said a prayer to Allah, and she was warned off. When the prince returned home, he told the king what had happened. The king was so furious that the wazir had left his son, he called him to his court and slew him.

The Good Ogre of Egypt

Now, to stigmatize all ogres as ravenous cannibals would be unfair. In the Egyptian tale "The Ostrich and the Sultan's Son" our perceptions and biases of the ogre are challenged. This tale first appeared in Hasan M. El-Shamy's 1999 collection *Tales Arab Women Tell and the Behavioral Patterns They Portray*, but the author claims that the story has existed for generations. It begins similarly to "Puss-in-Boots" but with a gender reversal. Three sisters, having lost their parents, each inherited three hens. God felt bad for the youngest daughter, since she was deprived of her parents at such a young age,

and gave her hen a specific gift: the ability to lay "gem eggs." This made her sisters jealous and they decided to lower her hen onto their neighbor's property. Their neighbor happened to be an ogre.

The sisters claimed they had nothing to do with the hen's disappearance and helped their distraught sibling come up with a plan to get it back. They lowered her into the ogre's yard but then took back the rope and left her, which was *not* part of the plan. The ogre appeared and said, "Do I smell the odor of a human not of our race?" Instead of eating her, he demanded that she be his daughter. Not sure what else to do, she agreed. While in his service, she fell in love with the boy next door (on the other side of the house), who was the son of a sultan. Looking out a window that opened onto his property, she spoke with the son's ostrich who warned that the ogre was surely fattening her up to be eaten. The girl relayed the ostrich's message to the ogre, who told her to tell the ostrich this: "He will raise me, [fatten me up to marry the sultan's son], he will make your feathers into brooms for me, your blood into henna for me, and your skin into a strap for my clogs." The ogre spoke the truth and the girl married the sultan's son.

Traditional Japanese Noh theater uses masks to depict characters such as monsters and ghosts.

What's In A Name?

In Japan, the stories of Onibaba and the Adachi-ga-hara and Mount Adatara regions associated with those tales have inspired three Noh plays. *Adachigahara* (or *Kurozuka*), *Dōjō-ji Temple*, and *Aoi no Ue* (or *Lady Aoi*). While *Adachigahara* recounts a reasonably straightforward version of the Onibaba legend, the other two offer very different interpretations of the ogress.

In *Dōjō-ji Temple*, the ogress is a vengeful shape-shifting spirit named Kiyohime who was once the daughter of a nobleman. She fell in love with a traveling priest who always told her that one day she would be his wife. By the time she had come of age, the priest no longer desired her. Distraught, Kiyohime chased him to the bank of the Hidaka River. The priest managed to cross it by boat, but Kiyohime had to swim. As she struggled, she turned into a giant serpent. The priest continued to Dōjō-ji Temple and hid under a bell, but the giant serpent was able to track his scent. She coiled herself around the bell, turning it white hot, and burned him to death.

In *Aoi no Ue*, the ogress, Lady Rokujō, is a vengeful spirit, more akin to a ghost, but the connecting thread between her, Kiyohime, and Onibaba is vengeance, despair, and the physical battle that can occur when a woman is driven mad.

THE OGRE WILL ALWAYS BE WITH US

"I'm not a demon! I'm a human being!"

ACTRESS NOBUKO OTOWA, *ONIBABA* (1964)

T HE OGRE HAS BEEN PRESENT IN MYTHS AND lore the world over since mankind began telling stories centuries ago, and the creature is no less prominent today than it was when Charles Perrault first put pen to paper or when Homer first wrote of the Cyclops in his epic tale, the *Odyssey*. The multi-media world in which we live has also allowed this creature to stay alive.

FOREIGN POP CULTURE

In 1964, Japanese director Kaneto Shindo completed his film version of the Onibaba legend. Although entitled *Onibaba*, it offers up a completely original story. In feudal Japan, two women

Opposite: Actress Nobuko Otowa depicts the title character in *Onibaba*.

living in the wilderness ambush and kill passing soldiers for their armor and trade them to a local merchant for food. One day, their neighbor, a young man, returned from war and told them the husband of the younger woman was killed. He proceeded to seduce the young woman. This made the older one jealous, so she donned a mask taken from a fallen samurai she had killed to scare the younger woman away from her new lover. But doing so during a rainstorm, she found the mask had bonded to her face. Desperate, she disclosed herself to the younger woman and explained what she had done. The younger woman managed to break off the mask with a hammer only to discover that her friend's face was horribly disfigured. She assumed that she had been changed into an onibaba—or horrid creature—and fled. The older woman chased after her and both plunged to their deaths over a cliff.

Was the older woman an ogre? In a sense, yes. By all accounts she transformed into one when she put on the mask and plotted against her comrade. The physical change was a result of her actions—her submission to evil—which is in keeping with the Japanese perception of the creature.

The Original Shrek

Perhaps the most well-known modern-day ogre is Shrek. However, Shrek was not a creation of DreamWorks Studios but rather a concept built in the mind of children's book author William Steig. In 1990, Steig published *Shrek!*, which told the story of an ugly monster who marries an ugly princess. Since its publication, the book has been eclipsed by the incredibly successful series of movies based upon it, and has escalated the green monster into a loveable hero.

The book itself, however, offers a purer and simpler story that is more in line with traditional fairy tales. It tells of an ugly and sheltered ogre named Shrek, who is even uglier than his ogre parents. One day they decide to kick him out as they feel it is time for him to go forth and cause destruction. Shrek is superpowered in a way; he can breathe fire, shoot beams from his eyes, and puff smoke from his ears. He takes pleasure in scaring all the people, animals, and even plants along his

William Steig

way. In his travels he comes upon a fortune-teller who tells him that soon he will encounter a knight, defeat him, and claim a princess even uglier than he. When Shrek arrives at a castle, he encounters a knight at the gates and easily defeats him using his eye beams. He then enters the castle and finds himself in a hall of mirrors. This is the first time he has seen his reflection. Seeing how hideous he is, Shrek is able to put things in perspective and appreciate himself. He then enters the chamber of the princess, who is, in fact, uglier than he is. He is delighted by the sight of her, and they are quickly wed.

The *Shrek* film series has become a monster unto itself, and a very successful one at that. There have been four feature films, seven short films, and two television specials. There was also a spin-off *Puss-in-Boots* feature film (2011) that loosely based itself on Perrault's original fairy tale.

The Modern Puss-in-Boots

The *Puss-in-Boots* film deviates heavily from the original Charles Perrault tale. Rather than having the cat defeat an ogre, Puss must

fight the giant called The Great Terror—but the "giant" is not what it might seem.

Perhaps the modern-day Puss-in-Boots tale differs as a result of the Shrek series. By the end of the series, ogres are considered generally nice and misunderstood creatures. The Shrek films have little connection to the Shrek book as well. While certain plot points may stay the same, the overall storyline is inconsistent. One of the more charming aspects of the entire series is the inclusion of, and almost metaphysical take on, the greater world of fairy-tale creatures.

Land of Orcs

While the Shrek films are extremely popular, they certainly aren't the only movies to feature ogres. Arguably more popular are *The Hobbit* and *The Lord of the Rings* series of films based on the books by J. R. R. Tolkien. Tolkien himself was fascinated by many creatures from legend and folklore. He loved fairy tales as much as epic works like *Beowulf*, which he translated from the original **Old English** text early in his career. From these sources, he gathered inspiration for his own works.

Both *The Hobbit* and The Lord of the Rings book series feature creatures not unlike ogres. In the books, they are called "**orcs.**" Tolkien describes them as more goblin-like in many cases; however, there are similarities between them and the traditional ogre. For one, orcs are towering, ugly creatures that enjoy human flesh. Likewise, the source of the word "orc" is "orcus," same as ogre. *Orcneas*, an Old English variant of the word, meaning "evil spirits," appears in *Beowulf*. If Tolkien used the epic as a source, *orcneas* likely helped create the monsters of his stories.

Today's role-playing games also feature ogres.

OGRES TODAY

Outside of films, ogres continue to appear in books, as well as games. A popular game, the basis for several books, is Dungeons and Dragons (D&D). It is a role-playing game featuring many different fantasy creatures—one of which is the ogre. In D&D, ogres are a sub-race of giants. They are very tall, heavy creatures with great strength. Other media also features ogres, and it is clear from their continued presence that ogres are here to stay.

STANDING THE TEST OF TIME

Just like vampires, werewolves, or zombies, the ogre has stood the test of time. From the folktales of old to the movies of today, the ogre represents a certain abject malice that pries at our very soul. It is the creature we fear becoming. It is the creature we already are. It is the creature we might someday be. Unlike his monstrous brethren, the ogre is often times the result of mankind's deep descent into spite and greed. One becomes an ogre because of his actions, not because of tragic **happenstance**.

GLOSSARY

antagonist The adversary (bad guy) in a story.

exorcism The extraction of a possessing soul by religious means.

Ghulah An ogress of Arabic folklore.

happenstance When something happens by chance.

oni Demon, also ogre, in Japanese.

onibaba Literally "demon-hag"; a character in Japanese folklore.

Old English The language spoken by English people in the middle ages, closer to modern German than modern English.

orc A fictional human creature akin to a goblin or ogre.

orcneas Old English for "evil spirits" or "monsters."

protagonist The hero of a story.

sentient Able to feel, see, hear, smell, or taste.

sovereigns Gold coins.

wazir A servant.

yōkai Japanese for "strange apparitions."

xenia The Ancient Greek custom of hospitality, which included guests and hosts giving gifts to each other.

To Learn More About Ogres

Books

Basile, Giambattista, and Nancy L. Canepa (trans.). *The Tale of Tales, or Entertainment for Little Ones.* Detroit: Wayne State University Press, 2007.

Betts, Christopher (trans.). *Charles Perrault: The Complete Fairy Tales.* Oxford, England: Oxford University Press, 2009.

Warner, Marina. *Once Upon a Time: A Short History of Fairy Tale.* Oxford, England: Oxford University Press, 2014.

Website

SurLaLuneFairytales.com
www.surlalunefairytales.com
This website features forty-nine fairy tales from different places around the world.

Video

Shrek Movie Trailer
www.youtube.com/watch?v=jYejzdBwvY4
The original movie trailer for Shrek.

Bibliography

"Book of Amos." BibleStudyTools.com. www.biblestudytools.com/bible/passage
.aspx?q=Amos+2:9-12.

"Book of Deuteronomy." TLDM.org. www.tldm.org/bible/Old%20Testament
/deuteron.htm.

Basile, Giambattista. "Il Pentamerone; or, The Tale of Tales." Burtoniana.org. Trans.
Richard F. Burton, burtoniana.org/books/1893-Pentamerone/index.html.

Basile, Giambattista. "The Flea." SurLaLuneFairytales.com. Trans. John Edward
Taylor, www.surlalunefairytales.com/pentamerone/5flea1911.html.

"The Clever Young Man and the Monster." Afripov.org. afriprov.org/index.php
/resources/storiesdatabase.html?controller=afriprovstorydb&task=display2
&cid[0]=156.

d'Aulnoy, Madame. *The History of the Tales of the Fairies*. London: T. Sabine, 1785.

El-Shamy, Hasan M. *Tales Arab Women Tell and the Behavioral Patterns They Portray*.
Bloomington, IN: Indiana University Press, 1999.

Hall, Lesslie, trans. "Beowulf." Gutenberg.org. www.gutenberg.org/ebooks/16328.

Homer. "The Odyssey." PoetryInTranslation.com, www.poetryintranslation.com
/PITBR/Greek/Odyssey9.htm.

"Kiondondoe and the Ogre." BlueGecko.org. www.bluegecko.org/kenya/tribes
/embu/stories-ogre.htm.

Knowles, Sir James. "The Legend of King Arthur and his Knights." Gutenberg.org,
www.gutenberg.org/files/12753/12753-h/12753-h.htm#chapter_iv.

"Ogre" entry, *Encyclopedia Britannica*. www.britannica.com/EBchecked/topic
/425894/ogre

Perrault, Charles. *The Complete Fairy Tales of Charles Perrault*. Trans. Neil Philip and
Nicoletta Simborowski. New York: Clarion Books, 1993.

Phillips, Ellen, series ed. *The Enchanted World: Giants and Ogres*. New York: Time Life,
1985.

Shrek. dir. Andrew Adamson and Vicky Jenson, 90 min, DreamWorks, 2001.

Index

About the Author

Luther Cross was born and raised in Topeka, Kansas. When he writes, it's usually about monsters.